Created to Prosper

Unleashing God's Supernatural Economy

Randal L. Cutter

New Dawn Publishing
9955 NW 31st Street
Coral Springs, FL 33065

New Dawn Publishing

All Scripture is the author's translation from Greek
(Nestle-Aland, 27th Edition & Textus Receptus) or Hebrew
(HMT-W4). All rights reserved worldwide.

Cover Art: altitudevisual © 123rf.com Used with
permission under extended license.

DEDICATION

To the One who helped me understand what
He had hidden in His Word;

With much appreciation for my wife, Dawn,
my family and my congregation,
all who have walked these truths out with me.

CONTENTS

PREFACE..1

INTRODUCTION................................3

1 A CREATION PRINCIPLE: FIRSTFRUITS....8

2 MOSES REGULATED THE TITHE.............25

3 THE MELCHIZEDEK TITHE......................40

4 THE BLESSING OF TITHING.....................46

5 MULTIPLYING THE SEED..........................52

6 LEARNING GOD'S FINANCIAL WAYS......72

7 CONCLUSION..82

ABOUT THE AUTHOR..................................85

ACKNOWLEDGMENTS

Thank you to the members of
New Dawn Community Church,
past and present,
for pursuing the Lord with me.

Thank you to my extremely well-read family,
who, while on a family vacation, got a surprise
proof-reading assignment.

Thank you to my friend in Wales, Mandy
(as well as everyone else there),
who heard me preach a message on giving
and asked, "Where's the book?"
Here it is.

PREFACE

Another book on Christian prosperity? As you walk the aisles of any Christian bookstore, or scroll through online Christian bookstores, you will notice the many different books on Christian prosperity. They cover virtually every conceivable angle of the topic at hand.

However, as you peruse those books, you will see few that approach the issue from the perspective of the creation principle, and even fewer—if any—that reveal a gem about tithes and firstfruits hidden in plain sight in the Hebrew verses of the Old Testament. You will also find few that will encourage readers to believe that their personal giving patterns actually impact the financial prosperity of the very region in which they live. For these reasons and many others, yes, this is another book on Christian prosperity.

This book is also accessible, relatively brief, and intended to present a short study on what God's Word truly says on this topic. The many other books that I pointed to above are available for encouragement and further study, but this one is intended to give you a solid base in your understanding of how God created us to prosper.

INTRODUCTION

"It's your fault."

I was so stunned by the words that echoed in my head, that I stopped pushing the dilapidated lawn mower across the lawn and just stood in the center of our front lawn.

Usually when I prayed, I wasn't interrupted in such an extraordinary way. I had just been letting the Lord know that things were tough financially, and I didn't think that it was fair that people in the community in which I lived could have so much, even while I was failing to make ends meet with a very meager salary.

Of course, the last thing that I expected as I prayed was a divine interruption. At that point in my life, I wasn't even certain the Lord responded to prayer in such a personal way, and I most certainly did not expect Him to respond in a way that laid the blame upon me. But it certainly sounded like the Lord. The theological implications did not matter to me at that moment. I was so certain that it was not my fault, that indignation rose within me, and I blurted out, "What do you mean it's my fault?" The next words cut through my indignation with the sword of truth. I heard, as clearly as if the Lord were standing next to me, "You are the teacher."

As I heard those words, my mind opened in a way so that I could see clearly just exactly why it was my fault. It wasn't pleasant.

I instantly saw the great privilege that the Lord had given me. He had called me to become a pastor in a denomination that believed the Word of God so precious, that the seminary required all its students to learn the original languages in which the Bible was written before they could attend the seminary. The seminary wanted its students to grasp the original nuances and intent of the original languages as students digested His truth. This required taking three years of ancient Greek and two years of ancient Hebrew before entering the seminary. Then Greek and Hebrew training continued in the years at seminary. The seminary did all of this so that its students would be equipped to correctly handle the Word of Truth.

I had labored learning the Greek of the New Testament and the Hebrew of the Old Testament and had excelled at both. But just having the tools doesn't mean much if you don't use them. The Lord showed me, in a moment, the many times I had declared that stewardship, the management of our financial resources, didn't interest me. He showed me the many times when I had chosen to simply parrot the denominational teachings on stewardship rather than determine what the Bible says with the tools He had so graciously given to me. My refusal to learn what the Scriptures said on the topics of stewardship and prosperity had released poverty into my life.

As I stood in my front lawn, I knew one thing with absolute certainty, I was guilty. I had been given a great opportunity to use my God-given tools, and I had shirked that responsibility.

I don't remember if I finished mowing the lawn that day, but I do remember that I repented, and that I resolved in my heart to correct this great error on my part and begin a focused study on what God's Word says about financial stewardship.

What I learned not only changed my life, but also changed the lives of the members of my congregation, and the finances of the congregation itself. The turnaround in our congregational finances was so radical that representatives from the denomination eventually asked whether I could write a study on stewardship. They hoped that what had happened in my congregation could be replicated in others across the denomination.

While that request was never completed, primarily because the Lord was directing me out of the denomination at the time, I continued to see the benefits and power of my study unleashed in my own life and in the lives of the members of my congregation, even as we launched into a new Christian stream.

Of course, this book is the result of that study. Though the Lord first confronted me about this topic over thirty years ago, I have continued to grow in my understanding of God's financial plans for His people. The truths that the Lord first revealed to me have stood the test of time, and He has continued to lead me on a journey of discovery as I have mined the Word for His truth.

Through all the years, I have known that I would eventually write a book about what God has shown me. It is obvious that I have not been in a hurry, but of late I have felt the Lord prompting me to put to print what He has shown to me.

This book is the result of His prompting, and it reveals God's creative plan for unleashing prosperity into our lives. That plan starts in the very first chapters of the book of Genesis and unfolds into amazing fullness in many of the books of the New Testament. It reveals a path of life and power to those who are willing to step into His plan. It reveals the way that we can live in a supernatural economy that is far above the currents of our natural economy.

1

A CREATION PRINCIPLE: FIRSTFRUITS

The quickest paths to spiritual and economic poverty are those that ignore the firstfruits principle of giving. Our primary example of this truth is Adam and Eve. While living in paradise, they refused to bring a firstfruits offering to God. As a direct result, they lost the image of God and brought sin and death into the world. When I first understood this truth, I realized that firstfruits offerings are extremely important. If all the pain and suffering of our fallen world can be attributed to this failure on Adam and Eve's part, we must understand how to avoid this very same trap today.

Before we discuss how the command not to eat of the tree of knowledge of good and evil was a firstfruits offering, we must discuss creation principles. As we look at the creation account found in the first chapters of Genesis, we can find truths about how God intends this world to function; theologians call these truths *creation principles*. God built creation principles into the very framework of creation. Those principles still function today. If we follow them, life works out better for us. If we disregard them, our lives will not work as well.

Many of the creation principles deal with our physical universe. The Lord established physical laws at creation which still apply to our reality today, though the fall into sin has certainly had an impact on them. While I can imagine that God created the laws of entropy at the very beginning of creation, I can also imagine that His manifest presence in a perfect world provided the necessary energy to keep those laws from causing decay. In the same way, other physical laws that still govern our universe were certainly impacted by the fall into sin when God's presence no longer balanced them.

Likewise, the Lord has established moral and relational laws that are also intended to bring order to our universe. Such creation principles govern marriage, procreation, the relationship between a husband and wife, family, dominion over and care of the earth, and many other essential areas of our lives.

The creation principle that must draw our attention here is the one that governs firstfruits giving. Firstfruits giving is a creation principle, though it is not referred to as firstfruits giving in the creation account itself. The first chapters of Genesis certainly describe this principle, as we shall see, but they do not give it a name in those chapters.

Before we continue, we should clearly define what firstfruits giving encompasses so that we are able to recognize it in the first chapters of Genesis. Firstfruits giving is revealed to us in other Scriptures apart from the creation account. The book of Leviticus is one place it is mentioned.

> Then Yahweh[1] spoke to Moses saying, "Speak to the sons of Israel and direct them, 'When you come into the land which I am giving you, and you reap its harvest, bring the sheaf of the firstfruits of your harvest to the priest.'" (Leviticus 23:9-10)

As its name implies, a firstfruits offering was the first thing that was given to the Lord at the harvest, before any of the farmer's needs were met. We can learn three things about firstfruits giving in this passage. First, it was

---

[1] This is the Lord's given name (known as the Tetragrammaton). It is often translated LORD or Jehovah in different versions of the Bible, but is pronounced, "Yahweh" (or "Adonai" in Jewish circles).

given every time there was a harvest. Second, it was given in a sacrificial way before the needs of the farmer were met. Third, since the rest of the crop had not yet come in, it was a statement of trust in the goodness of God to bring the rest of the harvest in.

We learn one more important aspect of firstfruits in the book of Exodus.

> **Bring the first and best of the firstfruits of your land to the house of Yahweh. (Exodus 23:19)**

This passage shows us that a firstfruits offering wasn't just the first part of the harvest. It was also intended to represent the best of what was available. This was a reminder that God deserves our very best at all times.

With these important insights, we can now more fully define what a firstfruits offering is:

1. It is given first from a harvest.

2. It is the best of what is available at the beginning of the harvest.

3. It is a sacrificial offering given before the needs of the individual are met.

4. It is a statement of trust in God's provision for the rest of the harvest.

With that understanding, we can now see the commands which God gave to Adam about giving in the light of what we know about firstfruits offerings.

Though it is not called firstfruits giving in the creation account, we can clearly see that the pattern of giving God established in Genesis 2 is an example of giving firstfruits.

> **Yahweh God commanded Adam saying, "From all the trees of the garden, you shall surely eat, but from the tree of the knowledge of good and evil—do not eat from it—for in the day you eat of it, you will begin to die, and then you will die." (Genesis 2:16-17)**

We are told something about all the trees in the garden a few verses earlier, that they were **"pleasing in appearance and good for food" (Genesis 2:9)**. They were certainly among the best things in the garden, if for no other reason than God chose to highlight how wonderful they were. In addition, the tree of the knowledge of good and evil had a perceived edge over all the other trees.

The woman saw that the tree was good for food, and that it was pleasing to the eyes, and that the tree was desirable to make one wise, she took from its fruit and ate, and she also gave it to her husband who was with her, and he ate. (Genesis 3:6)

The tree of the knowledge of good and evil, just like all the other trees, was good for food and pleasing to look at, but in addition, it was also desirable to make one wise. In that way, to Eve, it held an advantage over every other tree.

We can now see that Adam and Eve were most certainly commanded to give firstfruits offerings to the Lord. The tree of the knowledge of good and evil qualified as such an offering for these reasons:

1. A firstfruits offering is given first from a harvest: The entire harvest of the tree of knowledge of good and evil was given to the Lord.

2. A firstfruits offering is the best of what is available at the beginning of the harvest: The tree of knowledge of good and evil held a perceived edge over the other trees. It was best in Eve's eyes because it also offered wisdom.

3. A firstfruits offering is a sacrificial offering given before the needs of the individual were met: The entire harvest of the tree of the knowledge of good and evil was given to God as a sacrifice of praise even though Adam and Eve felt they needed more wisdom.

4. A firstfruits offering is a statement of trust in God's provision for the rest of the harvest: By giving the harvest of the tree of the knowledge of good and evil, Adam and Eve proclaimed their dependence on God for wisdom.

With these insights, we can now see how firstfruits giving comes to us from the very foundations of our created world. It is most certainly a creation principle, which means it is a principle that governs the lives of all the inhabitants of the earth. As stated above, if we follow the creation principles, life works out better for us. If we disregard them, things do not work out as well.

Since every inhabitant of planet earth is subject to this firstfruits principle of giving, we must define it more fully, especially since most of today's inhabitants no longer live in an agrarian setting, and thus we must apply it to our lives in a much different setting than the one in which Adam and Eve lived.

Firstfruits in a Fallen World: Cain and Abel

We can now see how Adam and Eve were commanded to give firstfruits offerings to the Lord. When they failed to do so, the world became a far different place, but it was still governed by the original creation principles. When we understand this, we can understand the account of Cain and Abel from a new vantage point.

> **So, it happened as time passed that Cain brought an offering to Yahweh from the fruit of the ground. But Abel, he also brought from the firstborn of his flock and their fat portions. Yahweh looked with favor upon Abel and his offering, but He did not give attention to Cain and to his offering. So, Cain become very angry, and his face fell. (Genesis 4:3-5)**

Cain was a farmer who raised crops, and Abel was a shepherd who raised sheep. As a result, Cain brought offerings from his crops, and Abel brought offerings from his flocks. The fact that they both gave offerings to the Lord indicates that they knew about the firstfruits creation principle. They had received no other command from the Lord, and yet they both brought offerings.

This is critical for our understanding of how firstfruits offerings are given in a fallen world. The only command that Cain and Abel had received about giving offerings to God was the same one that Adam had been given. While the tree of the knowledge of good and evil was now off limits, as was the entire garden in Eden, they could still follow the creation principle of firstfruits giving. That meant that they needed to give the first and the best, and they needed to give it in a sacrificial way that demonstrated trust.

It is obvious that Abel's offering did exactly that. Abel offered the firstborn. The firstborn among animals is the firstfruits of the flock. When a domestic animal gives birth to its first male offspring, it is cause for celebration. This is a promise for the future. This male animal would now be able to breed offspring and assure the strength and continuity of the flock. Sacrificing such an animal makes no sense, and yet it is a clear application of the firstfruits principle. It was first, and it was sacrificial. In addition, Abel also sacrificed the fat portions, the portions of his animals that were considered the best. As this story unfolds, the human author of Genesis, Moses, makes absolutely certain that we understand that Abel is following the creation principle of firstfruits. He could not have made it clearer.

He also could not have made it clearer that Cain was not offering firstfruits. While Abel brought of the first and of the best of his flocks, Cain merely brought an offering. The lack of descriptive qualifiers speaks volumes, especially when compared to Abel's offering. Cain was giving superficial obedience to the firstfruits principle without the true sacrifice that firstfruits requires. As a result, the Lord did not give any attention to Cain's offering. It did not meet the criteria for an acceptable offering.

Pay attention to that last sentence. If there is a creation principle that still governs our giving patterns—and there is—it means that some of our offerings are the type of offerings that God looks upon with favor, and there are some that fall short of what is necessary to gain His attention. That fact should get our attention.

It is even more important when we see what the apostle John says about Cain in 1 John 3.

> We are not like Cain, who was from the evil one and brutally murdered his brother. Why did he murder him? Because his activities were evil, and his brother's activities were righteous. (1 John 3:12)

Note that John is comparing Cain's actions against Abel's actions. The only activities that we have on record are their giving activities. Abel's offering activities were righteous, Cain's were evil. The only command that had been given by God about giving was the firstfruits principle. When Cain violated the firstfruits principle of giving, his offering activities were considered evil.

This demonstrates even more fully why we need to get this right. Violating the firstfruits principle is clearly very serious.

Giving Firstfruits in a Non-Agrarian World: Tithing

Long before Moses penned instructions from the Lord to Israel about tithing, the Patriarchs were applying the firstfruits principle of giving when they gave tithes. We see this especially in the lives of Abraham and Jacob.

While Abraham, as a man who kept herds, certainly followed Abel's example of giving the first and best in a sacrificial and trusting way, we also have an example of how he applied the principle when there were other types of wealth involved in the harvest. We see this when Abraham rescued Lot and the people of the city of Sodom from the four kings who had plundered them.

When Abraham returned with the spoils of war, he was met by Melchizedek, king of Salem and a priest of God. Although there is another section of this book which delves more deeply into what we can learn from this offering to Melchizedek, I am simply showing here how Abraham interpreted the firstfruits principle when he gave an offering that didn't come from fields or flocks. We read in Genesis 14:20 that Abraham "**gave him a tenth of everything.**" Abraham was following the only command that God had given to that time, the firstfruits creation principle. He applied it by giving ten percent of the spoils, a tithe, to Melchizedek.

That certainly helps us understand how we can apply this creation principle to our own lives today. Abraham is called the father of faith. When the father of faith gave an offering to God that wasn't based upon the animals in his household, or the crops in his fields, he gave ten percent. This one example, as I will explain more fully later, certainly alerts everyone who walks in the faith of Abraham that we can appropriately apply the firstfruits principle by giving tithes, ten percent of our income, to the Lord.

However, this is not the only example that we have. Although we do not have any specific example of Isaac giving an offering that was not of the field or flock, and do not know how he applied the principle in a non-agrarian setting, we can gain insight through his son Jacob's vow on this subject.

After Jacob had fled from his brother Esau, God met him with specific promises about his future. In view of God's amazing grace in his life, we can learn much from Jacob's response in Genesis 28.

> **Then Jacob made a vow saying, "Since God will be with me, and He will watch over me on the this road that I am walking, and will give me bread to eat and clothes to wear, and since I will return in peace to the house of my father, and since Yahweh will be my God, then this stone which I have set up as a pillar will be a house of God, and all that You give to me, I will give a tenth to You."**
> **(Genesis 28:20-22)**

In the context of looking forward to everything he would ever make, Jacob defaulted to the same way of giving firstfruits that Abraham had used. When Abraham was confronted with wealth from a source other than the birthing of herds or the harvests of fields, he gave ten percent. In the same way, when Jacob could not foresee how the wealth would come, he defaulted to ten percent.

When we attempt to ascertain the will of God on a matter, the principle of first mention is important. When we observe how a topic is first used in Scripture (its first mention), it helps us discern the will of God on that subject more accurately. These "first mentions" of the tithe predate the Law of Moses by hundreds of years, and are clearly applications of a well-known giving principle, the firstfruits creation principle. This is strong evidence that the tithe has always been the way that God's people respond to the Lord.

Hidden in Plain Sight: Firstfruits and Tithes Equated

Many hundreds of years after the Patriarchs, as the history of Israel in the time of Hezekiah was being recounted, the Lord hid a reference to the fact that the tithes and firstfruits were equal in the understanding of the Israelites.

By that time in Israel's history, the Law of Moses was in effect. As we will be reminded later, we do not give because the Law of Moses enjoined the Israelites to do so. In fact, we must not use the Law of Moses as our instruction on this issue. But we can learn about how those who spoke and wrote Hebrew understood the relationship between the tithe and firstfruits.

The hidden reference that reveals this relationship is in 2 Chronicles 31. It recounts the immense quantity of offerings that the Israelites brought to the temple at Hezekiah's command.

> **As soon as the command broke through *to the people*, the sons of Israel multiplied the firstfruits of grain, new wine, oil, honey, and all the produce of the field; they brought a great amount; a tithe of everything. (2 Chronicles 31:5)**

Hezekiah's command had urged the Israelites to bring their tithe for the priests and Levites to the temple. As we examine how the author reports the response to this command, he equates tithes and firstfruits. He does so by using a specific literary device called chiasm.

The Hebrew language, like any other language, often employs various rhetorical devices in order to communicate truth. Chiasm is very common. Chiasm refers to a literary pattern in which the author writes a sentence, and then repeats the parts of the sentence in reverse order using different words to communicate the same thing. It is a way that an author can give further insight to the meaning of his words and thoughts. In 2 Chronicles 31:5, the chiasm is used in an acrostic pattern and looks like this:

A   The Israelites multiplied

B   The firstfruits of grain, new wine, oil, honey, etc.

B   A tithe of everything

A   They brought abundantly

As you can see, the "A" parts of the sentence reflect each other, and the "B" parts do the same. In this instance, "firstfruits" and "tithes" are treated as synonyms (Part B). What this means for our study is that in the mind of the Hebrew writer of this verse, the two terms mean the same thing. In the understanding of the scribe who wrote these words (at the direction of the Holy Spirit), firstfruits giving is the same as giving ten percent of one's income to the Lord.

Although there is even more to say on this topic, especially as it relates to the tithe and the Melchizedek priesthood, things are already becoming abundantly clear. At this point, it is apparent that the creation principle of firstfruits giving also refers to tithing. This has been demonstrated by Abraham and Jacob, and also by the anonymous scribe who reported the response to Hezekiah's command.

It is also apparent that we have not made any use of the directives of the Law of Moses to make this point, and in fact, have dissuaded people from looking to the Law of Moses for direction on what to give. As we will discuss more fully in a later chapter, the Law of Moses is not our covenant. However, creation principles apply to all people of all time. That means that firstfruits giving is our standard. In our non-agrarian society dominated by currencies, firstfruits giving is demonstrated by giving ten percent of our income to the Lord.

2

MOSES REGULATED THE TITHE

If you are tithing because Moses commanded Israel to tithe, you are falling far short of what Moses commanded, missing the real reason Christians tithe, and robbing yourself of God's blessing.

Moses did not institute the tithe; however, he did multiply it and regulate it. We can learn about God's heart for people if we examine where he instructed the Israelites to give their tithes. So, while we do not tithe because Moses instructed us to do so—specifically because we are not under that covenant—we will look at the three tithes he commanded the Israelites to give in order to see a part of God's heart on display.

The Three Tithes of the Law of Moses

Even though Christians should not build their theology of giving from the Law of Moses, we can still learn much from those laws. Jesus taught the prophetic nature of the Old Covenant in Matthew 11.

> **"For all the prophets and the Law prophesied until John . . ." (Matthew 11:13)**

The Law of Moses has prophesied many things to the New Testament Church. We are not bound by the commands of the Law, but we can learn from it as it reveals God's heart to us. As we study the commands God gave to Israel about tithing, we can see God's heart for giving even more clearly.

The Old Covenant Tithes

Many Christians do not realize that God commanded the Israelites to give three distinct tithes. We often speak of the fact that God commanded Israel to tithe, but we usually speak of the singular "tithe" rather than the plural "tithes." Yet, it is clear from the Bible and from extra-biblical sources that the Israelites gave three different tithes.

We will look at specific Scriptures about each tithe in a moment. For the sake of clarity, I am including a quote from the Jewish historian, Josephus, because he provides valuable insight into how Israel understood the commands to tithe in the first century of this era.

> **Over and above these two tithes, which I have previously stated that you are to give every year, the one to the Levites, but the other to the feasts, you must bring in addition a third tithe every three years to be distributed to those in need, and to the women who are widows, and the children who are orphans. (Antiquities IV, viii, 22)[2]**

Other non-biblical sources also validate this understanding of three tithes (see Tobit 1:6-8). These extra-biblical sources do not have the authority of Scripture, but they do give solid evidence that the Jewish people gave three separate tithes. One tithe was for the Levites, the other was for the festivals, and the third was for the poor. As we look at the biblical evidence for each of these tithes, we will see that they reveal the type of giving patterns that bless the Lord. These tithes prophesy.

---

[2] Author's translation of the Greek text of Josephus.

Tithe #1: For the Levites

When most Christians think of Old Covenant tithing, they think of this tithe which the Israelites gave to the Levites every year.

> "To the sons of Levi, look, I have given all the tithe in Israel for their possession in exchange for the service which they do, the service at the tent of meeting."
> (Numbers 18:21)

The Lord then went on to instruct the Levites to give a tithe of what the people gave them to the priests (see verses 26-28).

This tithe reveals God's heart for those who make their living in ministry and ministry support roles. When the Lord set up the financial system of Israel, He made certain that those who worked in ministry roles would be well-compensated. At that time, the Levites comprised less than four percent of the populace of Israel, yet the Lord gave them ten percent of Israel's gross national product (GNP). Likewise, the descendants of Aaron, the priests, only comprised a fraction of one percent of Israel's population, yet the Lord gave the priests one percent of the nation's GNP through the tithe that the rest of the Levites gave to them. It is no wonder that the party of the priests, the Sadducees, became the wealthy power brokers of Jesus' day.

This Old Covenant tithe prophesies God's heart to us. God desires to bless those who make their living in His service. Even the Levites who were not priests, who served the Lord performing the sometimes-menial tasks of ministry support, were a part of the upper middle class of Israel. Likewise, the priests would have been among the wealthiest in the land. It is obvious that God is not stingy with His employees.

Paul revealed this same aspect of God's heart when he addressed the financial honor due to those who manage the affairs of the New Covenant church:

> The elders who manage well are worthy of double financial honor, especially those who labor in word and teaching. For the Scripture says, "Do not muzzle the ox while he is threshing grain," and "The worker is worthy of his wage." (1 Timothy 5:17-18)

The Greek word translated financial honor in these verses is a word which can either refer to granting someone respect, or very often it is about giving financial compensation. In this chapter, a chapter which is also about honoring widows financially, there is no doubt it refers to financial support of those who labor in the Word.

We extend honor to people when we compensate them appropriately. That is why Paul adds that the worker deserves his wage. These verses are clearly about financial compensation. Paul wanted those who received their income from directing the affairs of the church to receive generous compensation (double the standard of the time). He understood God's heart on the matter. He understood what this first tithe prophesied.

While we have freedom to set salaries according to the financial realities of our cultural and congregational life today, we certainly must understand God's generous heart toward those who make their living laboring in His vineyard. When we do, we demonstrate that we understand the prophecy of this tithe.

Tithe #2: For the Festivals

The Israelites gave the second tithe every year for the three great festivals in Jerusalem. Moses explained.

> **You will surely tithe all the crops from your seed, that which comes out of the field year**

by year. You shall eat it before the face of Yahweh your God in the place where He chooses His name to dwell. Eat the tithe of your grain, new wine, oil, and the firstborn of your cattle and your sheep so that you may learn to fear Yahweh your God all your days. (Deuteronomy 14:22-23)

When the Lord called Israel to the feasts in Jerusalem, He made certain they would be able to have a good time. He set aside ten percent of Israel's GNP to finance the fellowship which took place around His festivals. The infusion of so much food and drink created an atmosphere of celebration throughout the city. Pilgrims came to connect with their God and with each other, and the Lord generously financed the party through this tithe.

This festival tithe reveals the Lord's heart for fellowship and celebration among His people. No wonder Jesus provided so much wine at the wedding of Cana (see John 2:1-10). No wonder He was accused of being a drunkard and a glutton (see Matthew 11:19). No wonder the people of Corinth actually became drunkards and gluttons in their fleshly understanding of God's heart on this matter (see 1 Corinthians 11:20-21). God was not stingy when He provided for the fellowship of His people. He planned for big parties.

Modern congregational life can benefit as we apply this understanding of God's heart to it. Again, we are not bound by the exact amounts to give, or the timing of the gifts, as the Israelites were, but we can live in the understanding of God's purposes. It is obvious that God enjoys our celebrations, and He is not put out when we invest our time and resources in such celebration.

For this reason, I believe that good fellowship events are worth subsidizing. I came out of a church background that, for the most part, did not subsidize fellowship. As a result, I did not understand the importance of such celebrations. As I have experienced such events outside of my congregation, and as I have come to understand the Lord's heart on this issue through study, my heart changed. We now often throw parties for the various ministry groups in our congregation. We provide special food at these events that is varied and abundant. We have also invested in congregational picnics to make these events feel even more special. We are attempting to live God's love for celebration with His people, as this tithe prophesies it.

Tithe #3: For the Poor

This is the only tithe which Israel did not give every year. Moses instructed the Israelites,

> When you have completed giving all the tithe of your crops in the third year, the year of the tithe, then you shall give it to the Levite, to the foreigner, to the orphan, and to the widow, and they will eat it in your towns and be filled. (Deuteronomy 26:12)

The Israelites gave this tithe every third year. It provided for the Levites who were not on duty in Jerusalem, and for those who had need.

This tithe reveals the Lord's heart for those who through bereavement or relocation are stretched financially or impoverished. The Lord is concerned for the poor. The following proverb shows us the wisdom of giving to the poor:

> The one who shows favor to the poor lends to Yahweh; He will repay him the reward he deserves. (Proverbs 19:17)

The Lord is so concerned for those who have legitimate need that He views any provision made for the poor as His personal debt, and the Lord always pays His debts.

The New Testament Church has always understood this aspect of God. When the apostle Paul and Barnabas were beginning to minister to the Gentiles, the leaders in Jerusalem approved their ministry with one proviso, as Paul explained:

> **They only asked that we might remember the poor and respond appropriately, the very thing I have always been eager to do. (Galatians 2:10)**

The leaders of the Church understood the Lord's concern for the poor, and they reflected His priorities.

Most Christians clearly understand the importance of what this tithe prophesies. The Lord wants His people to help the poor. There are a variety of ways that congregations live this prophecy out today. Creative Christians have found many creative ways of providing for those in legitimate need without funding negative lifestyles. When we fund legitimate need, as congregations or individuals, we are fulfilling the prophecy of this tithe.

In summary, on average, each Israelite was required to give twenty-three and one third percent of their income every year in tithes. I believe that we, who are under grace, miss the opportunities which the Lord has given to us if we limit our giving to ten percent—a fact we will focus on in later chapters—since, if those under law were able to give not only their tithes, but also many other types of offerings, we who have a far better covenant can be at least as generous. Of course, all these tithes prophesy that God's people are called to be generous on many different occasions in many different ways.

The Danger of Following the Law of Moses

While we can look to the Law of Moses for its prophetic messages, as we have done above, we must not live under it. I have already stated that Christians who tithe because of the Law of Moses are robbing themselves of God's blessings. In fact, Paul states that they are falling away from the principle of grace in their lives and reverting to a covenant of works that no one is able to keep.

In Galatians 5 the apostle Paul warns the Galatians:

> **For freedom Christ has set us free. Therefore, take your stand and do not again become entangled with the yoke of slavery. Look, I, Paul, tell you that if you are circumcised because of the Law, Christ will not benefit you.**
>
> **I again testify to every man who is circumcised because of the Law, that he is under obligation to keep the whole Law. (Galatians 5:1-3)**

Please note that Paul is very clear. Those to whom he wrote could be circumcised or not as they desired. But if they were circumcised because they believed they were under the Law of Moses, that was a different matter. At the precise moment that they accepted the Law of Moses, they were required to keep the 613 commands of that covenant in order to receive the blessing that had previously been theirs by faith. They had removed themselves from the position of "by grace through faith" to the position of "by obedience to the Law of Moses."

In the same way, giving tithes does not obligate one to the Law of Moses. However, if one tithes because they believe they are under the Law of Moses, they have "become entangled with the yoke of slavery." The blessings of the New Covenant, which had been theirs by grace through faith, no longer apply to them in the same way. They are required to keep the commands of the Old Covenant to obtain the same blessing they once had by the grace of God. This is an appalling mistake for a Christian to make. It trades freedom in Christ for restriction under Moses.

In Galatians 5, Paul paints this mistake in stark terms.

Whoever is justified by law no longer operates connected to Christ. You have fallen from grace. (Galatians 5:4)

When any Christian decides to respond to the Law of Moses in order to seek God's blessing, they are no longer living their daily lives connected to Christ and His blessing. What was once theirs simply because of their relationship with Christ, must now be earned through obedience to the Law. That means keeping all the commands of the Law of Moses, including the prohibitions against wearing mixed fabrics, eating pork, working on Saturdays, and the hundreds of other laws found in the Old Covenant. This is not a beneficial trade.

Paul points out how foolish this was as he addressed the Galatians:

> **Are you this foolish? You began by the Spirit and now you want to finish in the flesh? (Galatians 3:3)**

In his mind, it was the height of foolishness to enjoy the blessings of Christ and of the Spirit of God, and trade it all in for a legalistic existence that cannot possibly replace what we once had.

If anyone wants to live under the Law of Moses, that person must begin to give on average, twenty-three and a third percent of their income every year in order to fulfill the Law of Moses. They must also keep over six hundred other commands to enjoy the blessing in Christ they already possess by grace through faith.

On the other hand, if we recognize that our obedience is a result of God's saving work in our lives and that it does not earn God's favor, since Jesus already did that, we can tithe and give over-and-above offerings to our heart's content. In fact, it is the Spirit-inspired response of the children of God for all that our Savior God has done for us.

Of course, since God has tied specific promises to our giving patterns, we will see His promises fulfilled when we give; but we give as a response to God's great love for us, not in an attempt to earn His favor. Again, Jesus already won the Father's favor for us.

3

THE MELCHIZEDEK TITHE

Abraham gave his tithe to Melchizedek to highlight his eternal priesthood. In order to fulfill the firstfruits principle in the same way that our father of faith did, we must also give our tithes to Melchizedek. So that we understand what this means, we need to learn more about Melchizedek.

Melchizedek was the priest of the Most High God. He was also king of Salem, which means "Peace." When Abraham went to war against the four kings that plundered Sodom, Melchizedek, whose name literally means "King of Righteousness," met him on his return. I can't imagine how God could have telegraphed any more clearly that there was something very special about Melchizedek. He was a king. He was a priest of God. His name means king of righteousness, and his kingdom was known as peace. We can understand why the writer to the Hebrews saw a clear connection to Jesus in this man to whom Abraham tithed.

We read of Abraham's encounter with him in Genesis 14.

> **Melchizedek, king of Salem, brought out bread and wine. He was a priest for God Most High. He blessed Abram and said, "Blessed be Abram by God Most High, Creator of the heavens and earth; and blessed be God Most High, who handed your adversaries into your hand." Then Abram gave him a tenth of everything. (Genesis 14:18-20)**

This rather mysterious encounter is another hidden part of God's plan to demonstrate the superiority of the firstfruits creation principle over the tithes of the Law of Moses. Melchizedek was a priest of God Most High. He represented the same God that Abraham worshiped. He brought bread and wine to Abraham. These are the emblems of spiritual fellowship. He also brought a blessing to Abraham. Abraham demonstrated his belief that they worshiped the same God by giving this priest a tenth of all the plunder. The fact that Abraham gave him the tithe signifies that Abraham recognized the

41

preeminent position Melchizedek held before God. He recognized that Melchizedek was authorized to receive the tithe on God's behalf.

While we can draw other conclusions from this encounter, it is more expedient to let the writer to the Hebrews comment on it. He has just written that Jesus is a priest forever in the order of Melchizedek (Hebrews 6:20), then he explains the position that Melchizedek held:

> **Without father, without mother, without traceable lineage, having no beginning of his days nor end to his life, but similar to the Son of God, he remains a priest without ceasing. Now you see how great this man was, to whom the patriarch Abraham gave a tenth from the best of the plunder.**
> **(Hebrews 7:3-4)**

The writer to the Hebrews is clear about Melchizedek. He was a priest of God, and greater than Abraham. When Abraham applied the creation principle of firstfruits giving to his encounter with Melchizedek, he gave the tithe to Melchizedek. He not only demonstrated that Melchizedek was one who could receive tithes on behalf of the God of Abraham, but he also demonstrated that Melchizedek's priesthood preceded the Law of Moses and ranks higher than the tithes found in the Law of Moses. Before Levi was born, or Aaron became the first High Priest, Melchizedek was receiving tithes.

The writer of the Hebrews makes certain that we understand that this tithe preceded Levi. He wrote,

> **On the one hand, the sons of Levi who receive the priestly office have a command in the Law to receive a tenth from the people, that is, from their brothers, even though they come from the loins of Abraham. But the one whose lineage is not traced from them received a tenth from Abraham, and blessed the one who had the promises. (Hebrews 7:5-6)**

The Law of Moses gave Levi the right to collect tithes from the rest of Israel. However, Melchizedek lived long before the Levitical priesthood was instituted. Since he represented God as His priest on the earth, the law of creation, the firstfruits creation principle, gave him the right to collect tithes, even from the father of faith, Abraham.

The writer to the Hebrews draws some conclusions based on this fact.

> **Now, without any argument, the lesser is blessed by the greater. In the case of the priests, men who face death receive the tenth, but in the case of Melchizedek, the tenth is received by the one who is certified as alive. (Hebrews 7:7-10)**

The fact that Abraham was the father of faith, and the fact that Levi would be authorized to collect tithes from Israel, did not cancel the fact that Melchizedek was authorized to receive tithes from Abraham, and thus even from the Levitical priests.

Melchizedek was greater than Abraham and all his descendants, save One. That One is spoken about in Psalm 110.

> **Yahweh has sworn and will not change His mind; you are a priest forever after the order of Melchizedek. (Psalm 110:4)**

While the Levitical priesthood has passed away, as can be expected of men who die, the order of Melchizedek lives on in Jesus Christ. Today, the family of faith gives its firstfruits as Abraham did, to the One who remains a priest forever in the order of Melchizedek. Since Jesus is God in the flesh, He certainly has the right, in and of Himself, to receive all that we can give to honor Him. However, He has also taken on a mantle which gives the one who wears it authority on this earth to receive tithes given in response to the firstfruits creation principle. As God and man, He has all authority to receive the tithes, and He continues to direct all of us to give our tithes to those who represent Him on this earth.

All of Abraham's seed, his descendants, gave tithes to Melchizedek through Abraham's offering. Now, the family of faith continues to give tithes to Jesus, who is the High Priest according to the order of Melchizedek. When we give to those who now represent Jesus, we are demonstrating the same faith Abraham showed when he gave his ten percent to Melchizedek.

4

THE BLESSING OF TITHING

How would you like to keep your cars, electronics, and appliances in good working condition, and only replace them when you tire of them rather than when they break down? There are several key promises in the books of Malachi and Haggai which can give us hope that such things are possible even today.

Although both books were written to people who lived under the Law of Moses, we can look to what God promised to those under the Law and realize that those of us who live under the New Covenant are able to live in those promises through Christ. Jesus fulfilled the Law perfectly. Thus, all the Law's promises are His, and through Him, ours.

You can also think of it in this way, if the people of Israel who labored under a covenant of obedience received such amazing promises, how much more those who live under the covenant of grace? These are promises to which we can attach our faith as we give. When we do that, we can also more accurately recognize when God is fulfilling those promises in our lives.

Malachi wrote specifically to the Israelites about tithing and the promises associated with it. We will first examine those promises in this chapter. Then, in a later chapter, we will explore the promises found in Haggai about forms of giving that go over-and-above the tithe.

Malachi's Perspective

Listen to how Malachi portrays the blessing associated with the tithes Israel gave.

> "Bring all the tithe into the treasury of My house, that there may be food in My house. Test me, now, in this," says Yahweh, the One who leads armies. "See if I won't open the windows of the heavens for you, and I will pour out blessing for you in unending abundance. Then I will rebuke for you all that consumes *your substance*. It will not destroy the fruit of your ground, and the

vine in your field will not lose *its fruit,*" says Yahweh, the One who leads armies. (Malachi 3:10-11)

The majority of Malachi's first readers understood farming at a very basic level. They understood that insects, blights, droughts, and various fungi could impoverish a farmer, and even a nation. There were always things that could devour a farmer's substance.

God's promise to the people of Israel was, first, that He would open the windows of the heavens when they tithed. To grasp the significance of the blessings this implies, we only need to turn to Genesis 7 to see how God first used the term He used here in this verse, *the windows of the heavens.*

In the year, the sixth hundredth year of Noah's life, in the second month on the seventeenth day of the month, on that day all the springs of the great primaeval ocean burst open, and the windows of the heavens were opened. (Genesis 7:11)

Because of this passage, when any Israelite heard that the windows of the heavens would be opened over them, they realized overwhelming floods of some kind were being released. In this way, God's specific promise in Malachi is that He would empty out the heavens and flood the people with His blessings until they could handle no more. That is an amazing promise for those who tithed.

Then, in another very specific promise, He stated that He would rebuke the common devourers in the lives of those who gave. Farmers feared drought, pests, fungus, raiders, and all of the many other ways their crops could be devoured. Can you imagine the hope this engendered in the hearts of His people as they heard this promise? It can engender the same hope in our hearts today.

Just as in Israel's day, we face many things today that devour our substance. There are always devourers. They attempt to consume our substance and abort God's provision in our lives. We can all think of the many unexpected expenses that come against our finances, often at the most inconvenient times. I mentioned only a few of them above.

But the incredible promise of God is that He has built pesticide into the very essence of creation. It keeps the things that devour at bay. That is how creation principles work. If we respect them, we walk in levels of safety. For instance, if we respect the creation principle of gravity, and don't throw ourselves off dizzying heights, we generally will walk in safety. In the same way, if we respect the creation principle of firstfruits giving, we can expect to generally walk protected from the things that devour. I say "generally," because of course, we do have an enemy of our souls who is always intent on stealing from us and harming us. If this book were about spiritual warfare, we would delve more deeply into stopping those illegal attacks. Suffice it to say, when we follow God's plan for our lives, we can use God's promises as an intercessory defense against anything Satan launches against us, and see Satan's plans defeated by our righteous Judge, Jesus.

Of course, Malachi's promises go much further than simply rebuking the things that devour. He also promises floods of blessing that will pour out from heaven into our circumstance. No wonder King David could confidently say:

> **"I have been young, and I am old, but I have not seen a righteous man forsaken or his seed requesting bread." (Psalm 37:25)**

David knew about these spectacular promises of God and lived in them.

Again, I must make it clear, we are not under the Law of Moses as Malachi and the Israelites were. We turned our attention to Malachi to note the many blessings that the Lord promised for following His plans for giving. When I recount the blessings of tithing, I always add the promises found in the book of Malachi since they are ours in Christ. In addition, if God could challenge those under the old covenant to test Him in firstfruits giving, and promised obvious blessing as a result, how much more should those who are under the covenant of grace also test Him in this area? He has most certainly given us permission to do so.

5

MULTIPLYING THE SEED

As we have seen, firstfruits giving is like a personal electric generator that releases power in our lives. There is another type of giving that reflects another creation principle. That principle is about sowing and reaping and applies to giving over-and-above offerings. If firstfruits giving is like a personal electric generator, sowing seed through over-and-above giving is like a nuclear powerplant.

While firstfruits giving has amazing promises, there is even more power released for more people when we give over-and-above offerings. When God's people sow generous offerings above their firstfruits, they will not only experience personal blessings, but the entire economy of a region can be impacted in a positive way.

Permit me to restate this in another way for emphasis: When we give ten percent of our income, it releases incredible power and protection, however, the most significant power is released when we sow seed offerings into God's purposes. By definition, seed offerings are those over-and-above offerings that we give beyond our firstfruits giving. As I wrote in the previous chapter, we will look at what Haggai wrote on this topic a bit later, but we will start with what the apostle Paul taught the Corinthians about God's plan for such over-and-above giving.

It is no surprise that the full power of sowing financial seed waited until the New Testament to be revealed. Giving patterns and promises needed to be touched by the power of the cross and Jesus' resurrection to achieve their full potential. The Law prophesies, but Jesus releases abundant life to us.

The apostle Paul reveals the amazing power of over-and-above giving in 2 Corinthians 9. As Paul addressed giving, he is clearly not replacing the well-known standard of firstfruits giving. In fact, in Romans he used the example of firstfruits giving to speak of God's promises to the nation of Israel.

> **Now if the firstfruits is holy, so is the whole lump of dough. If the root is holy, so are the branches. (Romans 11:16)**

He used this illustration from firstfruits giving to highlight a major truth about Israel. But as he did, he also highlighted a major financial truth for us. When we give firstfruits, all of our dough is holy (pun intended).

We all have a financial lump of dough. When we give firstfruits offerings our entire financial lump is sanctified and set apart for the Lord. This is the key that we need to unlock what Jesus said in Matthew 6.

> **"For where your wealth is located, your heart will also be located there."**
> **(Matthew 6:21)**

Jesus taught that the place you focus your wealth is also the location that you put your heart. That truth has potential to create a problem for believers today.

In today's economic reality, it is not unusual for people to put between thirty and forty percent of their income into their mortgage or rent. It is the largest expenditure in the budgets of many Christians. This may bother a sensitive conscience, since Jesus pointed out that we can find the location of our hearts by tracking where our money goes. No Christian wants to look at their annual budget and find that those budgets may indicate that their heart is financially centered on a house. Yet

Jesus stated that we can find the location of our hearts by where we direct our money.

The answer to this dilemma is found in firstfruits giving. If we are giving firstfruits, our heart isn't located in a house. If we are giving firstfruits, our entire financial lump is already sanctified for God's Kingdom purposes. The whole lump is holy (set apart for God), even the portion we pay for our home. If we are giving firstfruits, it is as if we are giving everything to God. In this way, all our wealth is focused on Him.

As we are about to see, this certainly doesn't mean that God has no plans for the rest of our resources, or that we don't need his input on our other spending plans. We need His continuing wisdom and guidance in all things in our lives. But it most certainly means that we can have confidence that when we give ten percent, firstfruits, God receives it as if we are giving Him everything we possess. Firstfruits giving centers our life upon the Lord and His Kingdom.

Paul's illustration in Romans 11 affirms the practice and importance of firstfruits giving through this illustration about Israel by showing us that firstfruits giving sanctifies our whole financial lump. In addition, in his second letter to the Corinthians, he examines the other creation principle that impacts our financial lives, the principle of sowing and reaping.

In 2 Corinthians 9, Paul mentioned this sowing and reaping creation principle as he discussed giving that is over-and-above firstfruits tithing. In this chapter of Corinthians, he has turned his attention specifically to the famine offering for God's people in Jerusalem. However, the same creation principles he outlined for this offering also apply every time we sow over-and-above seed into something.

We get to the heart of Paul's theology on sowing in chapter nine:

> **But know this, he who sows in a stingy manner will also reap a stingy harvest, and he who sows in a lavish manner will also reap a lavish harvest. (2 Corinthians 9:6)**

In this verse, Paul applied a physical creation principle to the topic at hand. When a seed is sown into the ground, it multiples. As a result, if a farmer sows seeds into the ground, he is able to reap a harvest beyond what he has sown. If a farmer sows a small amount of seed, his harvest will be smaller. If he sows more, the harvest will be larger. We all understand how this creation principle works, but Paul also applied this principle to what happens when we sow financial seed.

Since he is addressing a financial offering in this verse, he uses financial terms in his application of the creation principle. He equated sowing physical seed to sowing financial seed and pointed out that they work the same way. When we sow a financial seed, it multiplies just like a physical seed. If we sow a limited financial amount, it will still multiply, but because of the more limited number of seeds, it will not multiply as much as if we sow more seed. This is not a punishment, it just the way the creation principle works. In the same way, if we sow in a generous way, it will multiply into a generous harvest. In essence, if you want a big harvest, you've got to sow more seed.

Whenever I teach this principle, I take pains to point out something that Jesus said about a poor widow who donated almost nothing compared to the large amounts of money that the wealthy people were giving. Jesus said about her,

> "I am telling you the truth, this poor widow put more in the offering box than anyone else who gave an offering. All the rest gave from their expendable income, but she gave

even though she can't make ends meet. She gave everything; all that she had to live on."
(Mark 12:43b-44)

Thus, when we speak of sowing seed lavishly, or sowing a limited amount, we are not speaking only about the financial amount of the seed offering. We are also speaking of the relative size of the seed offering, that is, how costly it is to the person giving. In essence, God not only takes the amount of seed sown into account, but also the relative cost to the individual who sowed it.

For instance, if a billionaire sows a seed of a million dollars, for most of the rest of us, that is still a staggering amount to give (at the time I write this). However, in God's economy, depending on the percentage of a person's wealth that is being sowed, a gift of hundreds or thousands of dollars from a person who does not have as much resource may be the much more lavish gift. It all depends on the resources one has available when he or she gives.

I mention this to show that the wealthy do not have an inherent advantage in sowing seed. In God's economy, it is also about the cost to the individual. However, no matter the exact amount, when we sow, we can expect that the seed will multiply, and that we will reap a harvest commensurate to what is sown. The more costly what is sown is to an individual, the more the harvest will impact the person's financial well-being. If the seed sown is not significant compared to the resource the person has available, the harvest also will not be significant compared to the resources the person has available. If you want a return that impacts your bottom line in a significant way, you must sow a seed that is more costly in order to achieve that impact. That is how this creation principle works.

Of course, God is always interested in our hearts as we sow. His Kingdom is not just about our actions, but what is on the inside of us. Since Paul understood this, he also focused on the heart when he discussed giving. He demonstrated that we could give and receive offerings in a way that harms rather than helps our heart.

> **Each one, should do as he has decided ahead of time in his heart, not with a heavy heart or feeling pressure, for God loves a cheerful giver. (2 Corinthians 9:7)**

Seed offerings are not, nor should they be, about compulsion or duress. They should be about cheerful generosity. Paul's clear advice on how to achieve and maintain this cheerful mindset is to determine in advance the amount of seed to sow. This gives the person the ability to pray about the amount, and then take measured steps of faith in response to God's generosity in his or her own life.

In a very real way, the apostle is helping God's people become farmers who grow financial seed. In the same way that a farmer does not plant his field whimsically or emotionally, but only after clearly evaluating the condition of his field, his supply of seed, and how best to use it, so Paul directs Christians to make their plans ahead of time in order to take best advantage of appropriate giving opportunities.

As a result of this direction, when I am going to give an offering somewhere, I generally determine the amount I am going to sow before the offering has even started. On occasion, if I find out something I did not know about a need, I may adjust the amount upward. If I feel pressured, I will usually wait until after the pressure is lifted to determine how much I am going to sow, even if that means sending the gift later. This gives me freedom to enjoy the opportunities that God gives me to sow into His Kingdom on every occasion.

This is also a clear message to those who receive offerings. We must never take them in a way that causes stress or puts people under compulsion of some sort. Whenever I present a special offering opportunity, I strive to follow Paul's example. He shared the need. He shared the Scriptural promises. He even shared testimonies about how generously others gave. Then he gave people the time they needed to sow the seed.

We follow that same pattern in our congregation when we present an over-and-above need. We certainly share the need and the biblical promises, testimonies about God's faithfulness, and then we usually give the congregation the week to pray and meditate on whether they will participate or not—and, of course, at what level they will participate. My testimony to you is that I am always amazed at how generous the people of my congregation are as we follow Paul's outline for sowing over-and-above seed offerings. God does amazing things in the hearts of His people when we give them the freedom to go through this biblical process as they give.

These simple strategies have helped all of us learn to give with consistent cheerful generosity. That is the goal. Paul then added in the next verse.

Now God is able to make every grace overflow on you, so that in all things you always have all the things that you need, and

that you might overflow in every good work. (2 Corinthians 9:8)

He taught that when we are giving with cheerful generosity, God loves it, and He is able to make all grace overflow in our lives. That is an amazing promise. We all need more grace. This is evident from what Paul wrote. When grace overflows on us, we will in all things have all that we need for every good work. This is a promise that when I step forward to do some good thing, God will meet me with His grace so that I have exactly what I need to do it. That truth builds confidence for all the things that God has called me to do. You can easily see why it is important to give in freedom with cheerful generosity.

But Paul didn't stop there. If he had, it would be more than we deserve. But he continued by giving us even more motivation to keep on sowing seed with cheerful generosity.

The One who provides seed for sowing and bread for food will supply and multiply your seed and increase the harvest of your righteousness. (2 Corinthians 9:10)

We all have at least a rudimentary understanding of how farming works. The farmer sows seed that produces more seeds (grain). Some of that seed is for eating, and some is seed for sowing. Paul taught that God is the One who makes the seed available for sowing, and He is also the One who makes bread (seed that has been ground, kneaded into dough, and baked) available for food. The farmer must always determine what is seed to be sown and what is food to be eaten.

In the same way, God gives us financial seed to sow. When we see a return on it, we must think like farmers. We have to determine what part is further seed to be sown into a future harvest, and what part is able to be consumed on our needs. This is a basic part of farming. It must also be a basic part of our management of our funds.

Just as a farmer cannot consume the seed he must plant in the field, it would also be a mistake for us to consume the seed that God has given us to sow. As Paul stated, God's purpose is to multiply our seed, not necessarily our bread. I'm not saying that He does not want to multiply our bread, He certainly is generous and gives us good things. My point is that Paul emphasized the fact that God is interested in multiplying our seed so that we have even more to sow. This is an upward spiral in our Christian lives: the more we sow, the more seed we get to sow, and things keep increasing.

Now here is where it gets profound. Paul stated that as God multiplies our seed that is to be sown, He will also increase the harvest that we get from those seeds. What is that harvest? Righteousness.

Often when we sow seed, we think only of material returns. The next verse clearly promised those type of returns. But before we get to that verse, we must pause and consider, "What is a harvest of righteousness and how does it increase?"

To me, this is the most important part of Paul's seed promises. We all desperately need righteousness. If we are in Christ, we are declared righteous through His blood. That is what is called forensic righteousness. It is His righteousness applied to our accounts before God. But there is also applied righteousness in our lives. Paul wrote Timothy about it:

> "Flee from the passionate desires of youth, and pursue righteousness, faith, love, and peace, along with all those who call upon the Lord from a clean heart." (2 Timothy 2:22)

We apply the righteousness of Christ to our lives when we see it transformed into action in our lives. When we flee the often-misdirected passionate desires of our youth, and instead pursue righteousness, faith, love, and peace, that is evidence that we are experiencing a harvest of righteousness in our lives. Every one of us needs more of that type of righteousness in our lives. The truth is, when we do not have that type of applied righteousness at work in our lives, financial blessing can be a curse rather than a benefit. People who have abundant financial resource have the ability to indulge themselves in many pleasures, even sinful ones. The harvest of righteousness which Paul promises is intended to protect us from such self-harm as God blesses us. It is an important benefit, and an amazing promise, from sowing over-and-above seed.

After this important lesson on how God protects us from using our blessings incorrectly, Paul spelled out the fact that God does want to bless us financially as we give.

> **You are being made rich in everything, so that you can be generous at all times. Your generosity will produce thanksgiving to God through us. (2 Corinthians 9:11)**

Paul finally turned to the material returns we can expect when we sow seed. He has already stated this in verse ten, but also kept our eyes focused on the importance of distinguishing which returns are seed and which returns are bread. Then he wrote about the amazing harvest of righteousness. This harvest in and of itself will most certainly also help us distinguish between seed and bread, since it deals with the issues of greed in our lives. When righteousness trumps greed, we will not consume what God intends us to sow.

But now, in verse eleven, Paul wrote of being made rich in every way. While he certainly was speaking of the many spiritual blessings God pours onto His people—such as familial peace, and contentment in our journey of life—he most assuredly was also speaking of financial returns. In fact, he specifically stated that when we get the financial returns, it is not just so that we can revel in our wealth, but so that we can be generous whenever we need to be. That is the upward spiral God intends to unleash in our lives. The more financial seed we sow, the more financial seed we will have, not only to enjoy, but also to sow. This allows us to step into levels of generosity that most people rarely achieve.

I started this chapter by stating that the most significant power is released when we sow seed offerings. I think you would agree with this after reviewing all the things the apostle promised to us. Firstfruits giving certainly protects our resources and releases blessing, but sowing over-and-above seed actually multiplies our resources.

We serve an amazing God. He could just command us to do what is right and generous. But He is more interested in our hearts, and He has established the promises of the seed offering to encourage us to step willingly into cheerful generosity.

A Challenge to Believe Beyond our Own Circumstance

While I have understood the concept of seed offerings for a considerable time, like most people, I usually thought only in terms of a personal harvest in response to my giving. That means I saw the promises of sowing and reaping impacting the individual, and those in their immediate sphere, such as family and friends. In essence, I saw the promises as a personal electric generator giving power to me and my family. God changed my perspective on that back in 2010. He showed me that our over-and-above giving could make power available for our whole region. He taught me this by changing the economic circumstance in our community after showing us just how to do it.

In 2008, the county in which I live was one of the epicenters of that year's mortgage crisis. By 2010 many houses were empty, unemployment was over ten percent, and things were generally difficult. In response, early in 2010, the Lord challenged me to work on changing this dismal reality. When He challenged me, He pointed to seed offerings as the answer I would need.

We already knew that God had protected the members of our congregation who followed both creation principles on giving. We had not suffered loss in the economic collapse, and the majority of our members kept their jobs, or moved to even better ones. We also saw the power of over-and-above giving at work throughout that entire time providing power to each family so that they prospered through this difficult financial time.

However, we had no concept of the power of seed offerings to move our county into *supernatural economy*. But after seeing what happened in my county from 2010 on, I am a firm believer in the incredible power of seed offerings to change the very environment around us.

In one sense, this makes perfect sense. God's people are a city on a hill, a lamp on a stand. We are supposed to leak light and that light changes the darkness. On the other hand, I had not considered that our light could change the financial state of our depressed community. But I was about to learn this important truth.

In 2010, in response to the Lord's clear direction, I began to teach my congregation what the Lord had been showing me about our power to influence our economy through our over-and-above giving. Most of our members already understood the power of the seed to make us rich in every way, so it was a short step from our current understanding to recognizing that we could become rich in helping our community recover from its sorry state. We began to believe that God's supernatural economy could impact our county, and we began to act on that belief.

As a result, we began giving in a focused way. We started having a special seed offering Sunday once per month—a practice we continue to this day. It wasn't that people couldn't sow seed at any other time. In fact, multiple families do so many times a month. The purpose of seed offering Sunday was so that we would take the time to rehearse God's promises, and to believe that the seed we sowed would impact the county outside of our four walls.

On seed offering Sunday, we would rehearse what God had taught us, and then we would gather that Sunday's offering. While we usually take the offering buckets to a secure location immediately after the offering, we did not do that immediately on seed offering Sundays. Instead, we would bring them to the front of the congregation, and we would agree together in prayer asking the Lord to use it to change our community, and to do more than we could ask or imagine.

When we began to do this, we also diligently watched news reports to see the result in our economy. At the start of 2010, our county's unemployment rate was 10.2%. By year end it was down to 9.6%. That was a huge drop in such a short period of time for a county of two million people. But it did not stop there. From that time on, we saw the economic indicators in our county continue to improve at an astonishing rate. A year later, the unemployment rates was down to 8.7%. A year after that it was at 7.5%. Although we do not have abundant natural resources or an industrial economy, there were times our county led the nation in the recovery; and it just happened to begin at the point we began sowing seed offerings with a focused purpose to bring benefit to our county. At the end of this season of recovery, our county was in amazing financial shape, and had one of the lowest unemployment rates in the nation (under 3%).

I offer this anecdote, not only because I can present it as a divine strategy for the power of seed offerings, but also to challenge you to set your vision higher. As you grow in faith in this area, expect to see changes outside of the four walls of your community. God can certainly do abundantly more than we can ask or think. Our light is able to change our regions.

> **Now to the one who is able to do abundantly above all things that we could ask or think, through His power at work in us, to Him be the glory in the Church, and in Christ Jesus, unto all the generations, forever and ever. Amen. (Ephesians 3:20-21)**

6

LEARNING GOD'S FINANCIAL WAYS

When we walk diligently in God's financial plan, we release immense blessing in our own lives and in the lives of those around us; when we ignore our responsibility to learn God's financial ways, we can unleash material, physical, and spiritual poverty into our lives, and often into the lives of those around us. I started this book with the story of how the Lord graciously confronted me over the fact that I was shirking my responsibility to learn His ways and teach them to my congregation. I must add that I was tithing during that time. I had begun tithing very early in my Christian walk. So, I wasn't being disobedient in that arena, but because of faulty doctrines on this issue in our denomination, I also wasn't teaching my congregation to tithe.

My disobedience was grounded in not digging more deeply into God's financial plans for our lives so that I could apply them to my own life, and to the lives of those in my congregation. That disobedience resulted in a distressing lack of resources in our lives that impoverished my family and limited my congregation. I didn't realize it at the time, but God was communicating to me through my circumstance so that I would repent, change my behavior, and turn to His Word. He wanted me to do this so that He could release financial blessing to my family, my congregation, and my community.

I am so thankful that He intervened in this way. I am well aware that He did not need to do so. When the rich man who had ignored God's giving plan for his life died and arrived in Hades, he saw Lazarus with Abraham. The rich man was so distressed by his circumstance, and so concerned that his relatives would also end up in Hades, that he asked Abraham to send Lazarus back from the dead to teach them. Abraham's response revealed God's normal method of speaking to us.

> "But Abraham said, 'They have Moses and the Prophets. Let them hear and respond to them.'" (Luke 16:29)

Abraham's clear message is that God has communicated everything we need to know in His Word. However, in my case, He mercifully intervened in a personal way, not just for my sake, but for the sake of the thousands of people in the community. But Abraham's message to the rich man teaches us that we cannot presume that God will intervene in this way, especially when His will has been revealed in His Word.

As mentioned above, He can reveal many things to us through our personal circumstance. We often see this in the patterns of the Old Testament. We can learn much from this since, as we have already noted, the Law and the prophets prophesied until John (Matthew 11:13). That means that we can learn God's heart and many of His methods of communication by examining how He shepherded Israel.

When we turn to the book of Haggai, we learn a lot about God's financial methods of communication. While Haggai is written to those under the Law, and it has limited application to us, we can still learn much by listening to what the Spirit was prophesying to His Church today, even as He was speaking to Israel in the past. As Paul said to the Corinthians:

Now these things happened to them as typical examples, and they are written to admonish us, to whom the purposes of the ages have fallen. (1 Corinthians 10:11)

Paul's point was that we can learn how God deals with His people today from what is written about how He dealt with Israel in the past. With that in mind, we can profitably learn from what was written in Haggai.

Haggai Weighs In

The book of Haggai is about an opportunity for over-and-above giving. It isn't a book about God's plan for giving according to the Law of Moses. It is a book about how God wanted people to rebuild the temple that had been destroyed by the Babylonians a century earlier. He wanted His people to respond to the needs of His temple by giving special offerings so that it could be rebuilt.

In the same way today, there may be times that God intends to fund some project or outreach through our over-and-above offerings. Since He still gives us these same opportunities today, it is more than appropriate that we notice the ways that the Lord works to get the attention of His people, so that they will do what He is calling them to do for special offerings.

The problem that the prophet Haggai addressed, is that the Israelites did not pay attention to God's invitation to rebuild the temple. They did not see how they could afford to participate. However, Haggai let them know that they could not afford to ignore God's invitation. Haggai explained that God was attempting to get their attention so that they would step into this opportunity for a special offering:

> **But now, thus says Yahweh, the One who leads armies, "Set your heart upon your ways. You have planted much but gathered little. You eat but there is not enough. You drink but there is not enough to become drunk. You wear clothing, but you cannot stay warm in it. The one who hires himself out for wages puts them in a bag with holes." (Haggai 1:5-6)**

The first consequence of not following God's invitation to participate in their special project is that the Israelites did not reap commensurate to what they had sown. One can imagine the desperate farmers to whom Haggai was writing. They had diligently worked the fields expecting a harvest that would not only replenish their seed, but one that would feed their families for the next year. If a Jewish farmer in that day harvested little, they were walking on the edge of famine and disaster. As a result, the farmer and his family would never have enough to eat.

Haggai adds that their vineyards had provided so little, that they could not have gotten drunk if they wanted to do so. Of course, Haggai was writing to God's people. He certainly did not expect them to want to get drunk. His point is simply that there wasn't enough wine available to get anyone inebriated. It was in short supply since they had not followed God's plan for their finances.

In our day, we hear many of the same complaints that those farmers would have been making. It can feel like we never have enough, that we work long hours for little return, and that there is not enough money to make it from paycheck-to-paycheck. While God may use circumstances like this to help young Christians, and young Christian couples, to grow in their understanding of finances, it should not be the norm for His maturing people who have learned to exercise dominion over their finances. If this is in fact the case in your life, take a moment to agree with God that this is not His plan for you (it isn't), and ask Him to show you how to step into His purposes in your finances. It certainly starts with firstfruits giving, but then extends to sowing seeds as God gives us opportunity. Please be aware that if God sent Haggai to help a people who lived under an old covenant to understand this, you who live in the New Covenant may now be holding this book because He wants you to understand. He desires to help all of us.

God graciously sent Haggai to explain the negative impact of ignoring God's plan for their finances. The first result was a lack of prosperity, the second result was that their vitality was fading. Even though they were wearing clothing, they could not stay warm. It is as if they were experiencing some of the common frailties of old age even in their prime.

When King David was old, he experienced this type of frailty. He could not keep warm no matter how much he wore or how many blankets he used. The solution that his courtiers devised was to get a young woman to lie next to him as a heat source. This was not a solution for the common man in Haggai's time, nor would it be ideal for the young women of their age. However, God provided a much better solution to all these issues. The solution was to follow God's directives on giving toward the rebuilding of the temple.

It is often difficult for modern believers to comprehend that poor spiritual choices in our giving patterns can impact even our health. Yet Haggai makes it clear to the Israelites that this may be one way that God communicates, and since the Law prophesies to us, this can even apply in our era. When we violate any creation principle, there are many things that can be impacted negatively. Haggai simply makes this truth abundantly clear in the arena of sowing seed.

The third negative result Haggai's readers were experiencing, was that they put their wages into purses with holes. That is a vivid picture. No matter how much the people of Israel earned, it was as if their wallets had holes. No matter how much they put in their wallets, it seemed to leak right out.

While this condition could be caused by their many expenses, it can also be caused by a lack of self-control and wisdom. One of the great blessings of following God's plan is the fact that He releases self-control so we are not given to impulse, and He gives wisdom so that we spend wisely. In that way, the holes are patched and we can begin to build wealth.

While Haggai exposed the many ways that the lives of his readers were being impacted by their failure to follow God's leading about their finances, he also presented a major promise, not only to his first readers, but to us. If we change our ways, we can expect the Lord to respond. When Israel responded to Haggai, and followed the Lord's command, the Lord responded and said, **"From this day, I will bless you"** (Haggai 2:19).

Again, we do not live under the Law of Moses. The people of Haggai's day were called to participate in a special opportunity, the rebuilding the temple. However, we can learn the gentle ways of God by reading how He confronted those men and women of God when they refused this invitation. It is always appropriate when we have stepped into some form of financial distress to check our lives. Are we walking according to God's plan for giving in our lives? Have we lost sight of the firstfruits principle? Have we ignored an obvious invitation to be involved in a special project in our home congregation that God intends to use for our own congregation and for the community? Based upon the pattern we see in Haggai, these are very good questions to ask ourselves on our path to restoring financial wholeness to our lives.

I don't want to leave this quick study of Haggai without examining the unstated truths. All of the hardships that the people of Haggai's day were experiencing were aberrations. This was not supposed to be the way things worked. It is clear that Haggai expected that God's people would see their hard work bear fruit. He expected that they would be able to provide for their families. He expected that vitality would be released in their physical lives, and that God would plug the holes in their financial and material lives. In Haggai's mind, the Israelites only had to follow God's specific plan for them, and all would be restored to normal. God intends the same for us.

7

CONCLUSION

It is clear from our study, that those who teach that we should not tithe are not doing their followers any favors. The very first sin was a sin against firstfruits giving, and greed and poverty has been the result in the hearts and lives of humanity since then. When we give as God has commanded, we put the ax to the root of greed in our lives and unleash prosperity all around us.

This short study is intended as a quick start guide for God's people so that we can stay on track, or get back on track, in our financial understandings, and deal with any root of greed that attempts to control us. You can prosper as God intends, if you put God's plans into effect in your life.

This study has demonstrated that tithing is a creation principle which applies to all people of all time. It shows how the patriarchs, especially Abraham and Jacob, clearly understood how this principle applied. It has also demonstrated that a tithe was an appropriate firstfruits offering in non-agrarian settings. We also saw that the scribe who wrote down the words of 2 Chronicles 31:5 understood that tithes and firstfruits were equivalent. Giving ten percent of our income is the application of the firstfruits creation principle even for God's people today.

In addition, even though the Law of Moses no longer applies to us, we were able to see how the Law regulated and multiplied the tithing principle for the people of Israel. The people of Israel gave two tithes each year, and another every third year. While the Law directed how much to give and where it was to be given, the locations He chose for the tithes to go also prophesied God's heart in a way we can understand today. It revealed God's heart for those who serve Him in full time ministry, how important fellowship is among His people, and, of course, how important it is to care for the poor. We can still walk in the fulfillment of that prophetic understanding today as we direct our finances into areas that God's Law prophesied to us.

Of course, the real power in Christian giving is found in sowing financial seed. The promises that God has given His people are staggering and challenge us to see the impact of our giving not only in our lives, but in the very community in which we live. As we respond to the opportunities He gives us with cheerful generosity, He will pour out more than we can ask or imagine into our lives, and even into our communities.

All of these truths demonstrate that we serve a creative God, who has created us to give. As we do, we will see His Kingdom come in our finances on this earth, and we will see His Kingdom economy unleashed. He truly created us to prosper.

ABOUT THE AUTHOR

Randal Cutter is the founding pastor of New Dawn Community Church.

Randal is a dynamic teacher of God's truth. He has studied Greek and Hebrew extensively and informs his teaching with appropriate references. He has a theologian's perspective on biblical truth, and a pastor's heart for applying living truth.

In addition to his pastoral duties, he is also an Elder for the MorningStar Fellowship of Ministries, an organization that provides relational covering for ministries around the world. Randal has been an ordained member of the Fellowship of Ministries since its inception in 1995. In the past, he has also been an adjunct professor of the Greek language for MorningStar University's College of Theology. He has travelled extensively to teach the Word, and impart clarity, prophetic vision, and insight.

His first book, *Whatever You Bind on Earth: Authority Over Hurricanes*, has transformed the way that many in the body perceive authority in prayer. He has also published a translation of the New Testament titled, *The New Charismatic Bible: The New Testament*, available on Amazon.

Randal has been married to Dawn since 1980. They have three adult children, Alyssa, Linea, and Joshua, and two grandchildren.

You may contact Randal at:

New Dawn Community Church
9955 NW 31ST Street
Coral Springs, FL 33065
(954) 753-7729
NewDawn@NewDawn.org

You may see his current teaching messages at:
NewDawn.org

www.ingramcontent.com/pod-product-compliance
Lightning Source LLC
Chambersburg PA
CBHW062017040426
42447CB00010B/2033